M000235372

RETIREMENT
COMMUNITIES 101

RETIREMENT COMMUNITIES 101

What is a Continuing Care Retirement Community?
A Practical Guide to Understanding and Researching a CCRC

Dana Cornwell Bodney

© 2017 Dana Cornwell Bodney
All rights reserved.

Cover original watercolor, *Vignamaggio Vista* by Kate Cornwell
McGuire - All Rights Reserved

ISBN: 0692981071
ISBN 13: 9780692981078
Library of Congress Control Number: 2017917405
Createspace Independent Publishing Platform
Jacksonville, FL

The author and publisher do not assume and hereby disclaim any
liability to any party for any loss, damage, or disruption caused by
errors or omissions, whether such errors or omissions result from
negligence, accident, or any other cause.

For my children,
Kate and Ely

I promise to plan my future
so that you don't have to...
Love,
Mom

Acknowledgements

To Ty Morgan, Lisa Adams, Bernadette McAlphin, Sarra Ninya, Fritz Scholze, Kristi Quick and Bobby Sumner. Their intelligent minds and caring hearts continually contribute to the advancement and integrity of the senior living industry. Thank you for what you have patiently shared with me.

To my husband, Mike Bodney, for reviewing my manuscript countless times and offering editing advice. Thank you for keeping me on task with the question, "Why aren't you working on your book?"

To my son, Ely Cornwell, for encouraging me, "forever & always", in all areas of life and especially my writing endeavors.

To my daughter, Kate Cornwell McGuire, for generously gifting her art work for the cover of this book. Thank you for knowing my thoughts before a word is spoken.

Godspeed to all!

Table of Contents

Introduction

Researching retirement communities for yourself or a loved one can be very confusing. Most seniors will refer to this as their "last move". The heat is on to wade through all the options and information to choose the best community based on their individual situation and circumstances. Your research will include surfing the internet, calling specific communities of interest based on location and plans they offer, and visiting those communities to see for yourself if it is the one for you. It may sound overwhelming, but it doesn't have to be.

I am a retirement counselor at a Continuing Care Retirement Community (CCRC) and this book is designed to guide you through the selection process. It is a practical guide to understanding and researching a CCRC. The senior living industry is growing rapidly and new communities are popping up on ever other corner in neighborhoods across the country. The process of learning each community's admittance requirements, services offered and financial approval qualifications can be like going back to school again.

It can be a grand task finding the appropriate type of community to fit your needs and merely schedule an appointment. You may not even have any "needs" yet at all, but are simply trying to understand retirement options and plan your future responsibility.

Continuing Care Retirement Communities may be a very new concept for you to consider in your retirement research. A CCRC is a community which has all levels of care on the same campus. The journey begins in independent living and should a resident need more services or care, it is an easy transition to move to assisted living, memory care, or skilled nursing.

The questions you need to ask when considering a retirement community are in the following pages. You will learn new terminology and discover more options than you thought could exist for finding a solution in your new phase of retirement.

You will learn the difference between an entry fee CCRC and a rental CCRC. Entry fee communities offer a component called Life Care. It is a very beneficial option and synonymous with the term asset preservation and is a long-term care insurance policy.

Your journey at a CCRC will begin in Independent Living. Many residents make the move as early as possible, which is age sixty-two, just to enjoy the active lifestyle.

There are hundreds of CCRCs across America, each with detailed benefits associated with different plans for entrance and distinct standards of acceptance. That's right – acceptance. Health assessments will determine if a person is appropriate for Independent Living. There is a saying in the CCRC industry, "It is better to be two years too early than two minutes too late".

This book is a practical outline of steps to take to find the right community for you. It is designed to help you consider factors that may not have occurred to you and how they could affect your whole family. I will address pertinent questions you may want to consider as you visit different CCRCs.

The research process involved with finding the perfect community for you or your loved one doesn't have to cause anxiety. You will feel in control and less overwhelmed as you plan visits to communities you are considering for this important move in your life. Remember, all communities are structured differently. You are conducting your own research so ASK QUESTIONS. There are many general questions listed in the workbook section of the book for you to ask the retirement counselors at each community.

Retirement Communities 101 is an easy read and more like a narrative than a text book, so we will have some fun along the way. I do not claim to be an expert on the extensive CCRC industry, but I can promise if you use my suggestions your road to peace of mind will have fewer bumps.

Dog ear the pages – mark up the margins, highlight paragraphs and draw circles around topics of greatest concern. Do your due diligence and you will find the community that it right for you! Let's get started.

Blank space throughout the book is intentional so that you can make notes as you read.

Welcome to Retirement Communities 101

What is a Life Care CCRC?

A Life Care CCRC offers long-term living arrange-ments and health services in exchange for an upfront entry fee from the resident. A resident moves in at the independent living level. The Life Care Residency Contract is much like a long-term care in-surance policy. There are many benefits to a Life Care plan. The main benefit, in my opinion, is the Care for Life Guarantee which gives the resident peace of mind in the world of financial uncertainty. Should your assets be depleted, from no fault of your own, or you simply out live your assets, you will not have to leave the community. The residency contract remains in effect and the resident will continue living at the community. The community will hardship the differ-ence between what the resident can pay each month and what they should pay for services rendered.

Other benefits for the Life Care resident is access to healthcare services right on the same campus. Depending on the plans offered at a community the resident may or may not have monthly fee increases as they move to higher levels of care. If the fees do increase, the Life Care resident will pay significantly less than market rate. Discounts may be as much as 50% for nursing care and 30% for assisted or memory care. Those discounts are set at each community and referenced in the contract you will sign when you pay your entry fee.

Entry fees are paid at a Life Care CCRC to secure benefits and to theoretically buy down the amount of your monthly service fee. Typically, an apartment or home at a Life Care CCRC will cost less each month than one of equal size at a rental CCRC. The monthly service fees in independent living include many services like housekeeping, transportation, use of amenities, linen service and meals.

Life Care contracts vary from state to state and from community to community within each state. Although each Life Care plan is governed by a state statute it is never safe to assume that two plans offer the exact same benefits. I advise keeping a list of pros and cons for each community. One Community might appear to offer a better financial set-up at first glance. But, after a closer look you realize they have add-on charges for every little service, while a second community is more all-inclusive. Perhaps paying the slightly higher monthly fee is more cost efficient in the long run and offers the best solution for you after all.

Understanding Plan Options
at a Life Care CCRC

ndustry wide, there are three contracts for consideration at a CCRC.

- Type A Life Care contracts include housing, service and amenities with unlimited healthcare services available at no increased cost each month. Typically, these entry fees are the most expensive because the CCRCs financial risk is the greatest as a resident needs higher levels of care.

- Type B or modified Life Care contracts also include housing, services and use of amenities, but the entry fees and monthly fees are lower because the healthcare benefit is limited. The monthly fee will increase as the resident transitions to higher levels of care, but at a discounted rate from the market rate. Generally, the discounts are quite substantial.

- Type C is a fee-for-service contract. The resident fees still include housing, services and use of amenities, however when they need healthcare services they will pay the market rate.

Each community you visit will most likely have different contract options. Rely on the retirement counselor to explain all the options in detail. Share your situation and circumstances with the counselor regarding family, career history, hobbies, finances, health and more so that they can better explain why one type of contract may be best for you over another. If the community makes the cut on your list, ask for a copy of the contract to review.

How Much Does a CCRC Life Care Community Cost?

Services, costs, benefits and other details vary from one community to another. Please understand how important it is to go over all the details at each community. Do not *assume* they are the same as the last community you visited. We all know what happens when you *assume* anything! Even communities owned by the same parent company may operate differently than one another.

When discussing costs and fees it is particularly important to look at each community individually. Some of the factors which determine the entry fee amounts are:

- Location of the community
- Scope of the services included
- Square footage of the apartment or home you have selected
- Amenities

As with all economic pricing – supply and demand will also apply to CCRCs.

If you are interested in the concept of Life Care and the Care for Life Guarantee which it offers, you most likely can find a community for which you qualify financially.

As an example, I have signed residents for a lovely studio apartment with an entry fee of approximately $90,000. I have also helped a married couple move into a 2700 square foot home under a 75% refund Life Care plan for $700,000.

There are many scenarios in between the two examples listed above. Our community has 16 different apartment floorplans and about 14 floorplans for the homes. Think of the possibilities! My community is located near the beach, so imagine the cost of that same studio apartment in a location that is more rural.

Communities may be all-inclusive or a' la carte. That will make a difference in the entry fee you see on the fee schedule. The retirement counselor should provide you with a list of services and amenities included in your monthly fee.

Age Qualifications

Most communities require a resident to be 62 years old to qualify for a Life Care contract.

Very few CCRCs offer a refund plan after age 82 or 85. The community where I work is one of the few which does not have an age limit if you want to choose a Life Care plan that carries a refund. Don't let that be a reason to wait on your move. Remember, there are physical underwriting requirements which must be met as well. One visit to the doctor coupled with a new diagnosis may disqualify you overnight.

Dana Cornwell Bodney

Notes

How Do I Know When To Move?

This is an objective question with a variety of answers. I usually get around to this topic with my prospects after I have built much rapport and understand their feelings as well as their situation. Here are some questions to ask yourself:

- Do you wake up every morning worried about your future and that anxiety plagues you throughout the day? Are you constantly playing out scenarios in your mind regarding health or financial events?
- Do you feel like money is flying out the window for home maintenance and there seems to be no end in sight?
- Do you feel socially secluded?
- Are you eating nutritious meals? Are you finding it hard to manage grocery shopping, meal preparation and cleanup? Or maybe you simply do not care what you eat at all.
- Have you done your research and believe in Life Care, but are just playing the odds

because you feel like you can buy yourself a little more "time"? You are in "great health" and are "not ready yet".

- Are you at a loss of where to start in the process of moving? Rather than explore options you ignore your need for a change and secretly feel inadequate.

- Have you cared for your own mother or father and don't want to leave that emotional experience to your own children?

- Do you feel that you want to be the person to select the community where you will live out your life... and not someone else?

- "Finances are tight and I just know I can't afford to leave my home that is completely paid for... my children need money. Why would I sell the family home? But, I am miserable here after my spouse has passed away."

- I am the sole caregiver for my spouse. What happens if I die first? Who will care for my spouse?

- My children have lives of their own and live across the country. It is selfish of me to put a burden on them to be responsible for my future care needs.

- I feel so alone. All my friends are passing away or can't drive any more so we do not see one

another. The days are longer than I can han-
dle...I sleep mostly.

If these thoughts sound familiar it is time to seriously
begin to chart your course for a move.

Are the Entry Fees Refundable?

Generally, each community will have two Life Care plans available for you to consider. Most of the time the only difference is the entry fee cost and how the refund is paid should a resident move away or pass away.

At the community where I am a Retirement Counselor, the Life Care Freedom Plan will yield a refund during the first four years. If a resident moves away the refund will go to them or if they should pass away it will go to their estate. Four percent of the entry is nonrefundable when the resident signs the contract as an administrative fee. The remainder amortizes at a rate of two percent a month, so after about four years the entry fee has amortized down to zero. The entry fee for our Freedom Plan is less than our Liberty Plan.

Life Care Liberty Plan carries a seventy-five percent refund. There is a three percent nonrefundable administrative fee upon signing the contract and two percent per month amortization. When that amount reaches seventy-five percent, the entry fee refund amount freezes. At any time in the future should a resident wish to move away or if they pass away – either the resident or their estate will receive a seventy-five percent refund. This is a high-level asset preservation plan and offers options to move and have a refund as life situations change.

Entry fee schedules are broken into first and second person fees. The second person fee for Life Care is minimal in the large scheme; generally, around $15,000. This is an economical reason to move when both spouses apply for Life Care together. Emotionally, it is best to move when you have each other to manage the transition.

Which Refund Plan Option Is Right For Me?

A Life Care plan with a high level refund is an estate planning opportunity to preserve assets and in most cases will have the highest value at the end of a resident's life. Should you decide to relocate - your refund will be available and you will have more options in deciding where you would like to go. If these factors are important to you a high level refund plan may be your main focus. Review the contract for details on how and when the refund is disbursed.

A plan that amortizes down to zero after time, at a specific rate each month may be right for you if you never plan to relocate. For example, Jim and Joan Smith have lived in Jacksonville, Florida, all their lives and do not plan on leaving at this point. Paying the higher entry fee to ensure a 75% refund if they should decide to relocate is not appealing.

However, Marsha and Ben Jones are moving from Chicago, Illinois, to a CCRC in Jacksonville, Florida, to be closer to their son and his family. A 75% refund plan would allow them to relocate should their son have a career change and leave the area. Another consideration to choose a high percentage refund plan would be when one spouse passes away, the remaining resident may choose to move away from the community and closer to family in another part of the country. There may be other personal situations you should examine and talk over with your spouse and family as you consider your choice.

Life Care promotes asset preservation and a high refund plan is often a resident's choice, simply to fund their estate upon death and ensure an inheritance for their family.

What are the Financial Qualifications for Life Care?

The underwriting process varies from community to community. The prospective resident will be asked to fill out a financial form listing assets, liabilities, monthly income and long-term care insurance details if applicable. The underwriter will need to know if you are drawing down on investments to provide a portion of your monthly income, and what portion of a pension or other investments will pass through to the survivor upon the death of a spouse.

Assets will include your home and all other real estate you may own. You probably know the value of your property already, but consult a realtor or a website like zillow.com or trulia.com to verify the market value.

Long-term investments include mutual funds, stocks, bonds, annuities, certificates of deposit, IRAs and other financial holdings. Short-term bank accounts should be listed as well; like checking, savings and money markets to name a few. You can list other assets like an art collection, jewelry, or other items of value if you can provide a recent appraisal.

Liabilities might include mortgages, a home equity line of credit, credit card debt, auto loans, or any other loans of that nature.

Most communities would like for you to list on the form the expenses which you will have after you move to the community. So, expense items that apply to your primary residence, like lawn service or home insurance and taxes, need not be listed here if you are planning on selling that home. The underwriter is evaluating what your expenses will be after you move to the community.

If you have a long-term care insurance policy now is the time to pull it out of the file cabinet and review the benefits. You will want to list the amount it will pay per day in assisted living and skilled nursing. How many years does the coverage last or is it based on a maximum payout amount? What is the compound inflation protection rate on the policy? Is there a waiting period before you will begin to receive your benefit pay-out?

Verification of assets and income are necessary to accompany the financial form. Copies of investment and bank account statements, CD's, appraisals, etc. are generally accepted. A copy of your checking account statement is the best way to verify your income.

Prospective residents may opt to have a financial advisor or family member assist them in filling out this form if it seems overwhelming. It is valid information a CCRC needs to review to determine the best plan for a prospective resident. The prospects signature is required on the form to submit for application.

Once you submit the form the financial director at the community or their staff will review and begin the qualification process. Again, all communities are different, but here is an example of a qualification computation.

In this scenario, the entry fee is going to be $200,000 and the monthly fee for two people will be $4,000. A factor of 1.5 is multiplied by the entry fee amount of the apartment or home chosen by the prospect. The underwriters would prefer that the prospects have 1.5 times $200,000, or $300,000, remaining in their financial portfolio after they pay their entry fee. So, the level of qualification for this size apartment or home on the asset tab is $500,000.

Moving to the income qualification, it is a simple 1.5 times the monthly fee of the apartment or home. So, the underwriters would prefer that a couple's income is 1.5 times $4,000, or $6,000 a month.

Just so you remember .... Let's say it all together .... "ALL COMMUNITIES ARE DIFFERENT"! These are broad qualifying factors. In most circumstances, computation adjustments which include a mixture of asset and income information is sufficient to qualify for Life Care. An example would be a prospect who does not meet the asset requirement, yet greatly exceeds the income requirement. The approval process is not written in stone. It is wise to discuss the financial qualifications early in your research process so that you are aware of your options of apartment or home floorplans. Generally, the greater the square footage of the dwelling – the higher the entry fee. Remember, you are down-sizing! If you are tight in qualifying financially, take advantage of a lower entry fee on a smaller apartment. The common areas belong to the residents so you can always enlarge your living area by simply taking a walk.

Health and Physical Approval

"It is better to be two years too early than two minutes too late." I have mentioned this phrase already and now I am going to drive the point home. If you wait until you "need" to move to a retirement community, you will most probably not be approved for Life Care. You may be approved for a plan with little or no health care benefits or a fee for service plan, but not for Life Care.

Several years ago, I had the opportunity to work with a couple in their mid-seventies to discuss moving to my community. At the time, they would have qualified financially and physically. They dismissed the idea of a move at that time and gave me the classic cliché - "We're not ready". Fourteen months later, the gentleman called to tell me he was ready; he "needed" to move now and sign a Life Care contract. He explained that his wife had been diagnosed with Alzheimer's and the disease was progressing rapidly.

Unfortunately, I had to deliver the news that he had missed the opportunity to qualify for Life Care. He and his wife would still be able to move to our community under a Choice Plan, but the offer of our long-term care insurance policy would be denied due to her diagnosis. There would be a possibility for him to qualify for Life Care, but that application would be reviewed on a case by case basis by our underwriters.

During our initial meeting over a year ago, I explained the importance of good physical health to qualify for Life Care. This couple had chosen to roll the dice a little longer and stay in their home. That decision did not work out well for their retirement plan. This happens from time to time with prospects and it is painful to see the look of regret in their eyes.

Had they not waited until the disease was in advanced stages we could have perhaps offered them a Life Care contract. Each application is reviewed on a case by case basis. We ask the prospect to sign a form allowing their doctor permission to answer our questions about their health. This includes any diagnosis the prospect may have and medications they are currently taking. The form is reviewed and a health and physical assessment is scheduled. This is not an examination. It is a meeting with our Resident Services Director that will last about a half hour. If it is a couple it may take an hour. During the meeting you will discuss information listed on the doctor's report. There will probably be cognitive questions asked as well.

Now, with financial and physical underwriting complete, the Executive Director and his team will move toward final approval of the applicant.

Notes

Should I Be Worried That I Will Not Be Approved?

Time is of the essence to be approved for the plan which carries the most health care benefits.

On your initial visit to the community ask them what their financial and physical approval process entails. Remember all communities are different. If your financial situation and health assessment fit within guidelines of that community, you should not have to worry about acceptance.

If your personal health or financial qualifications come up short, do not assume that you will not be accepted. Most administrations will work with applicants to find a plan that will fit both their needs and their wallet. The retirement counselor should be able to give you a good idea of your chances for approval if you will share with them a snapshot of your assets, income and overall health status.

Most CCRCs will not accept an applicant who is not a resident of their community into their assisted living, memory care or skilled nursing. Make the move before you need these higher levels of care.

Some larger CCRCs do have rehabilitation facilities and respite care options for nonresidents. Should you have either of those care needs, choosing a CCRC may prove to be a good experience to familiarize yourself with the community. Some respite care patients are so impressed with our community they choose a Life Care plan and move straight from their assisted living apartment into an independent living apartment – without even going back to their home.

How Do I Know Which Life Care Plan is Best For Me?

After examining refund options and financial qualifications, as we have already discussed, you may be close to a decision. Ask the retirement counselor you are working with for their professional opinion regarding your specific situation.

The CCRC where I work has a financial qualification model that helps the future resident compare the value of their estate under each plan at the statistical time of their death as projected by actuarial tables. In the case of a married couple – upon the death of the second spouse. This very useful tool will calculate the life expectancy of the resident, based on age and gender; also, the number of years they will most likely spend in independent living, assisted living and skilled nursing.

Assets, liabilities, and income information are entered in the model spreadsheet, along with the entry fee cost and monthly service fee of the specific home or apartment the future resident has chosen. If the applicant has a long-term care insurance policy, details of the policy like the daily rate benefit, number of years covered under the policy or maximum pay-out amount, plus an inflation rider, if any, are also entered in as data.

The model will calculate the present value of accounts from which an applicate may be drawing down on for income and it will calculate the future value of assets as well. It accounts for increases in monthly service fees from a cost of living prospective and for those incurred from higher levels of care. The future resident will be able to see a projection of expenses and the value of their estate for each year in their actuarial life table. They can compare the estate value at end of life, between plans to help determine their choice.

What is a Rental CCRC?

A rental community will not offer the Life Care component. A rental CCRC generally has some or all levels of care, but make certain they are located on the same campus. There is an upfront administrative fee, usually less than $5000, and then a monthly service fee. The monthly fees at a rental community are generally higher than those at a Life Care CCRC for the same size apartment or home. Remember the upfront entry fee at a Life Care CCRC is buying down your monthly fee just as a down payment on a mortgage would lower your monthly payment.

A simple mathematical equation will reveal that after a few years in a rental community there is a breakeven point at which time it would have been more feasible to have chosen an entry fee community over a rental community.

There is no Life Care Guarantee at a rental community. If your assets are exhausted, you may have to leave the community.

Notes

Contracts

Read the contract through and mark sections that you feel need further clarification. Have a family member review with you or ask your financial advisor to look at the contract. The contracts are long, but straight forward. Call the retirement counselor back and ask specific questions. There should be an official "closing" where you sit with the director of finance or executive director of the community and go over each paragraph of the contract. After the contract is signed and executed – you are a resident!

Notes

Financial Advisors

Do not assume that your financial advisor understands all the benefits of a Life Care policy. It would be in your best interest to schedule a conference call between your financial advisor and the retirement counselor or the director of finance at the community. If your advisor does not understand how Life Care can preserve your assets the entry fee amount may raise their eyebrow. You are not going to find many financial advisors who are encouraging their clients to withdraw assets from their accounts without an in-depth explanation of WHY!

This meeting will show your advisor in his own language how Life Care can yield a higher end-of-life estate value, plus shield your children from having the responsibility for your health care costs should you out live your assets. I don't care how long you have had your financial advisor, or how much you trust him – he will not recommend Life Care to you until he completely understands the contract. After he does, he will be recommending it to all his clients.

Notes

Monthly Fee Increases

Every community will most likely increase the monthly fees in January. Try to select a community that has a cap on those increases. Our community's contract states that we can never increase fees more that 2% above CPI (consumer price index). If there is no cap on the increases – proceed carefully and insist on an explanation as to why there is none.

In either case, ask for the history of monthly fee increases for the past five years.

Notes

Long Term Care Policies
Plus Life Care

A long-term care policy can be difficult to understand. Most financial directors at CCRCs will help you understand the benefits if you are having concerns about coverage since you bought it years ago. As a courtesy, our financial director will meet with the prospective resident and conference call the insurance company to confirm their benefits. Then she will help the prospect understand how our different plans will interact with their policy to optimize their health cost coverage for the future. Your retirement counselor can assist with understanding long-term care benefits as well, so bring it along on one of your visits to each community as you narrow your search.

Life Care offers discounts on higher levels of care and the assurance that you will never have to leave the community if you out-live your assets from no fault of your own. Long-term care insurance policies will pay out monies to the insured for a certain length of time for covered services. Generally, it is a monthly or daily rate up to a maximum amount. When the maximum benefit pay-out for the policy is reached, the insured's coverage will end. Life Care ends only when a resident passes away or moves away. The peace of mind component is ever present with a Life Care policy.

If you have long-term care insurance and want to move to a CCRC with Life Care, do not cancel your long-term care policy. When the two are used in conjunction with one another the resident will have maximum coverage in the aging process, as well as, peace of mind for themselves and their families.

On-Site Wellness Clinic

On-site wellness clinics are a huge benefit to the residents. New residents may be relocating a substantial distance away from their doctor and need to ensure that upon arrival they will have immediate care if needed. Once they are moved in and settled they may opt to keep the on-site physician as their main doctor or choose from others in the area outside of the community.

In either event, maintaining a connection with the on-site physician is helpful and convenient to the resident when small matters pop up. In our community, the same on-site physician makes rounds in our assisted living, memory care and skilled nursing centers. Establishing this relationship early on in your residency at a community ensures familiarity with the doctor and his staff on a first name basis. As you transition through the levels of care it is comforting to know that the physician has watched you in your own environment with knowledge of how the community operates. A plus for your family is that there are no transportation appointments to set. You simply walk down the hall to the clinic – or better yet – they come to you.

Notes

Personalized Living & Home Health

A CCRC should have a department to assist their residents with activities of daily living on an as-needed basis. The services available may span from dog walking and insulin shots to medication reminders and showering assistance, and many more helpful personalized tasks in between. These are out-of-pocket expenses and the charges are gauged to fit the task.

Residents usually can remain longer in their independent apartments or homes where monthly fees are less with just a small amount of extra help from these community associates.

Some long-term care insurance policies will cover home health. Ask your retirement counselor at the community to review your policy.

Notes

Waiting Lists

Most CCRCs have a waiting list that is growing rapidly thanks to the baby boomers and the rise in cost for traditional long-term care policies. Typically, the fee to join the wait list is around $2000 or $3000, which is all refundable except a minimal administrative fee in the event you do not move to the community. If you do move to the community, the wait list fee should go toward your entry fee.

You will list several different types of dwellings, floorplans and locations within the community that you prefer to be notified about when they become available.

Learn the procedure of how each community's wait list operates. At our community, when your number comes up and you do not choose to move, you do not go to the bottom of the list; you stay in the same position. Some communities will place a wait list member at the bottom of the list after three passes.

Each month you may receive a packet from the Lifestyle or Marketing Department which includes the current calendar of events at the community showcasing events, social gatherings, fitness classes, seminars on various topics and a host of other opportunities for learning and engagement right on campus.

Most communities provide two complimentary meal vouchers per month so that you can enjoy the dining experience and get to know other residents. At our community, wait list VIP's receive name badges so that meeting, mixing and mingling with residents is easier.

A Side Note on Having the Right Mindset as You Research CCRCs

L et's take a moment to discuss personality types – amiable, analytical, expressive and driver. I am taking this short tangent so that you might identify yourself. Your normal purchasing styles that have been with you through life may have served you well thus far, but I have seen the negative side of buying traits keep prospects from making the right decision at the most important time.

- The amiable person is loyal, dependable and easygoing. These individuals do not want to deal with facts. Making decisions at all can be difficult for the amiable because they want peace and harmony and do not want to up-set anyone. The amiable person may be wishy-washy.
- An analytical person is organized and delib-erate. They want facts and documentation. Another trait for the analytical is being too

cautious. I have heard the phrase "analysis paralysis" used with this personality type.

- An expressive person is outgoing and charming; natural "people persons". They exhibit verbal skills and have good ideas but have trouble seeing them through to completion. The expressive person is less time-oriented.
- The driver is a results oriented individual. They are direct, decisive and usually talk fast. They may take risks to get results and are not detailed oriented. They view themselves as a leader and will make a decision even if it's the wrong one. They look at the big picture. They may be thought of as stubborn or arrogant.

Let's focus on the negative traits of these personality types: wishy-washy, analysis paralysis, slow to action, and stubborn arrogance. Don't let these traits hold you back from making important decisions for your retirement future. After you have done your due diligence don't let your emotional negative side keep you from moving forward. Keep taking the next step toward a secure and happy retirement choice.

Remember, if you fail to plan – you can plan on failing!

Complimentary Guest Stay

Ask your retirement counselor if they have a marketing guest suite for prospects to stay in overnight to get the flavor of the community. Have them arrange dinner with residents so that you can see the community from their point of view. One overnight visit is a mere snapshot of life at a retirement community. If you are interested in knowing more about the resident population, plan your visit around an event that is usually well attended.

Notes

Clubs and Organizations to Join?

Without a doubt, every CCRC will have many clubs and organizations for you to get involved with and meet other residents. The size of the community will be a determining factor on the variety and quantity of clubs and activities. Our community has over fifty clubs and organizations. Among them are croquet, woodworking, hand bells, golf, library volunteer, computer club, knitting, book clubs, Bridge, Poker, Bingo, community newspaper, aerobics, line-dancing, yoga, strength training, water aerobics, associate scholarship fund, Resident Council and much, much more.

Ask if the Lifestyle Director is open to suggestions from residents on new activities, events and organizations. It is important that you feel the community is your home and that your voice is heard regarding new ideas that may benefit other residents. If you have special talents or an interesting art collection or a passion for a non-profit organization – let the Lifestyle Director know and have them plan an event/seminar/class to share with your new resident family.

Notes

Moving Assistance and Downsizing Companies

This is a growing industry across America. Please check references to ensure a satisfying experience. Ask the community where you are moving who they recommend. Some communities may offer a move allowance if you use their preferred company since their track record of resident satisfaction is very high. The value of these companies out-weighs the cost. They can assist you with furniture placement, packing, moving, setting up your home or apartment and even arrange a complimentary guest stay at the community for a couple of nights while your new apartment is being set up.

Notes

Dining Options

This is a hot topic and many times part of the initial reasoning for someone to make a move to a retirement community. Cooking and grocery shopping have become a burden and nutritional health is suffering.

At a CCRC there are several different options for dining each day. Some communities have three or more venues and the resident can decide each day if they wish to have breakfast, lunch or dinner for their one meal a day which is included in their monthly fee. They may have the other two meals at the community, as well, and simply charge the cost to their account or pay cash in most cases. You should find the pricing very reasonable. Ask to see a sample menu from each restaurant, and about their hours of operation and dress codes.

Some communities offer a monthly meal allowance to be used at your discretion. Regular dining habits lead to better nutritional health. The one-meal-a-day approach is a better choice than the meal allowance in my opinion. A resident may deplete their allowance in the last week of the month and opt for less expensive and less nutritional choices.

Notes

Resident Handbook

Each community will have a resident handbook with very detailed information that you will want to review before you move to insure you are aware of specific procedures. You will find most answers to common questions in the handbook. Some may be quite lengthy, so request a copy via email.

· Notes

Pet Policy

Pets are allowed at most CCRCs, but there may be a size limitation. Ask what restrictions apply. A nonrefundable deposit is typical and may range from $400 to $600. Ask about the pet policy early on in your research at each community so you are not disappointed.

Notes

Other Topics To Research

- State statutes govern CCRCs. You should do an internet search to review the statute and see details on contracts and minimum liquid reserve requirements for each particular state where your community of interest is located.
- Review maps to determine the proximity of hospitals, shopping and other points of interest to you in relation to the community of interest.
- What is the overall financial viability of the CCRC?
- Is the CCRC engaged in the local community?
- Research specific cultural or lifestyle preferences which are important to you at each community.

Notes

Questions To Ask At A CCRC

This outline of questions will prove to be beneficial in recognizing the pros and cons of each community you visit. It will also help you to distinguish the differences between your top picks, so that you can narrow your search and choose the best community for you. Most communities will have handouts and brochures which they may give you to help answer the questions listed below (a site map, fee schedule, floorplans, dining room menus etc.) so that you don't have to write down all the answers. Once you are home you can compile the answers on your own spreadsheet. It need not be as fancy as an Excel spreadsheet – simply anything that helps you organize your research.

- Tell me about your community – size, age of community, number of homes and apartments, number of residents and number of employees.
- Do you have a waiting list or are there apartments or homes available now?

- Explain the different resident entry plans you offer.
- If the plan carries a refund – how is that paid out?
- What should I expect as I move to a higher level of care from a financial prospective?
- Explain the fees if one spouse is in a higher level of care and the other remains in the independent apartment.
- Do residents ever transfer to smaller apartments? Are there fees associate with a transfer and how does that effect my entry fee refund?
- How do you financially qualify a prospective resident?
- Can you help me understand which plan might be best for me and explain why, based on my personal circumstances?
- What information do you need from my doctor to approve me for residency?
- Are there certain medical diagnoses which could disqualify me for residency?
- Will you accept my long-term-care insurance policy (if applicable)?
- What services are included with each plan?
- Tell me about your dining options.
- Do I have to make a reservation or can I have my meals whenever I prefer?

- Do you have a dress code?
- Tell me about your transportation services.
- Tell me about linen services.
- How often will I receive housekeeping and what specific cleaning tasks are included? Which task might I be responsible for handling over time in my independent living apartment or home?
- Tell me about your fitness center and exercise classes.
- What types of clubs and organizations do you have at your community? (This would be a good time to tell the retirement counselor about your specific interests and hobbies.)
- Do you have church services on campus or transportation to those nearby?
- Do you have an on-site health clinic?
- What amenities do you have at your community? Do you have a library, pool, bank, gift shop, hair salon, work shop, art studio, or dog park? Whatever is important to you from that standpoint – ask specific questions.
- May I have over-night visitors and how long can they stay in my apartment or home? If they are my caregiver – can they stay longer?

- Which utilities are included?
- Are there emergency pull cords in each unit? Will I receive an emergency pendant?
- Do you offer personalized living services or home health?
- Explain your evacuation plan and procedure for acts of God – such as a hurricane – and other emergency action plans as might be pertinent in certain geographical locations.
- Where will I park my car?
- Tell me about your pet policy.
- Do you have any noise complaints?
- Do you have a resident counsel in place and how many residents are on the committee?
- What is the construction of the building – are there fire walls?
- If your apartment does not have a washer/dryer, ask how close the laundry room is to your apartment.
- What would be my first step to make a move to your community?
- Can you provide me with a timeline or checklist of required procedures to follow in making application for residency at your community?
- May I have a copy of your contracts via email?

- May I schedule an appointment to come back and tour your assisted living, memory care and skilled nursing facilities?

As you know, generally one question leads to another. This list will get you started on a thorough research path.

Notes

Schedule A Visit To A CCRC

You should consider visiting three different communities. Call ahead to schedule the appointment. If you or other family members have requested information via the internet or have called the community directly – let the retirement counselor know. You may already be in their database and that can save you some time with setting up the appointment.

Dropping by is acceptable, however, don't expect to get the full picture without allowing time to spend with the counselor. Their calendar may be tight already and there is not ample time to cover all the information. Remember, the retirement counselor is your best resource. Don't hold back information that is important to your retirement future. Ask questions and respond with answers when asked. The counselor may ask certain questions to guide the conversation so that you will have the best understanding of how the community can work for you. You may find that many of your questions are answered before you ask.

All the best to you in your search! Feel free to contact me at danacornwell@yahoo.com or visit my website danacornwellbodney.com.

Workbook

Community One

_____

_____

_____

_____

_____

_____

_____

_____

_____

_____

_____

_____

_____

_____

_____

_____

_____

_____

_____

_____

_____

_____

_____

_____

_____

_____

_____

Dana Cornwell Bodney

Community Two

_____
_____
_____
_____
_____
_____
_____
_____
_____
_____
_____
_____
_____
_____
_____
_____
_____
_____
_____
_____
_____
_____
_____
_____
_____

_____
_____
_____
_____
_____
_____
_____
_____
_____
_____
_____
_____
_____
_____
_____
_____
_____
_____
_____
_____
_____
_____
_____
_____
_____
_____
_____

Community Three

_____

_____

_____

_____

_____

_____

_____

_____

_____

_____

_____

_____

_____

_____

_____

_____

_____

_____

_____

_____

_____

_____

_____

_____

_____

_____

_____

About the Author

Dana Cornwell Bodney is a Retirement Counselor at a large CCRC in Jacksonville, Florida, near Mayo Clinic Hospital. She holds a BS Degree in Business with a Minor in Marketing from Clemson University in Clemson, South Carolina. Dana has a Real Estate Brokers License in Florida, South Carolina and Georgia.

Along with this nonfiction book, she has written Book One - *The Red Leaves of Autumn* - of a four-part fiction, mystery series. It is available on Amazon.com and Kindle. Follow the link:

amazon.com/dp/152324206X
or visit her website danacornwellbodney.com

Made in the USA
Middletown, DE
04 August 2021

45357520R00061